Mara and Friends

Ash Wants A Pet

Storybook

Claire Mark

All rights reserved

Copyright © 2020 Claire Mark

No part of this book may be reproduced or transmitted in any form or by any means, electrical or mechanical, including photocopying, recording, or by any information storage and retrieval system without permission from the author.

ISBN: 9798565067613

Cover Design and Publishing by Publishingbooks.biz

CONTENTS

Story Units

1. Friends say Hello	6
2. A Pet in a Basket	16
3. Kittens are Fun	21
4. What do Cats like?	24
5. Ash wants a Pet	26
6. Ash gets a Pet	30
Reading Comprehension	40
Art Project/ Story Retelling	41
Rhyme	42
cvc Words and Sight Words	43
Rhyme: /t/ and /d/	44
About the book...	46
Reading objectives fulfilled on successful completion	47

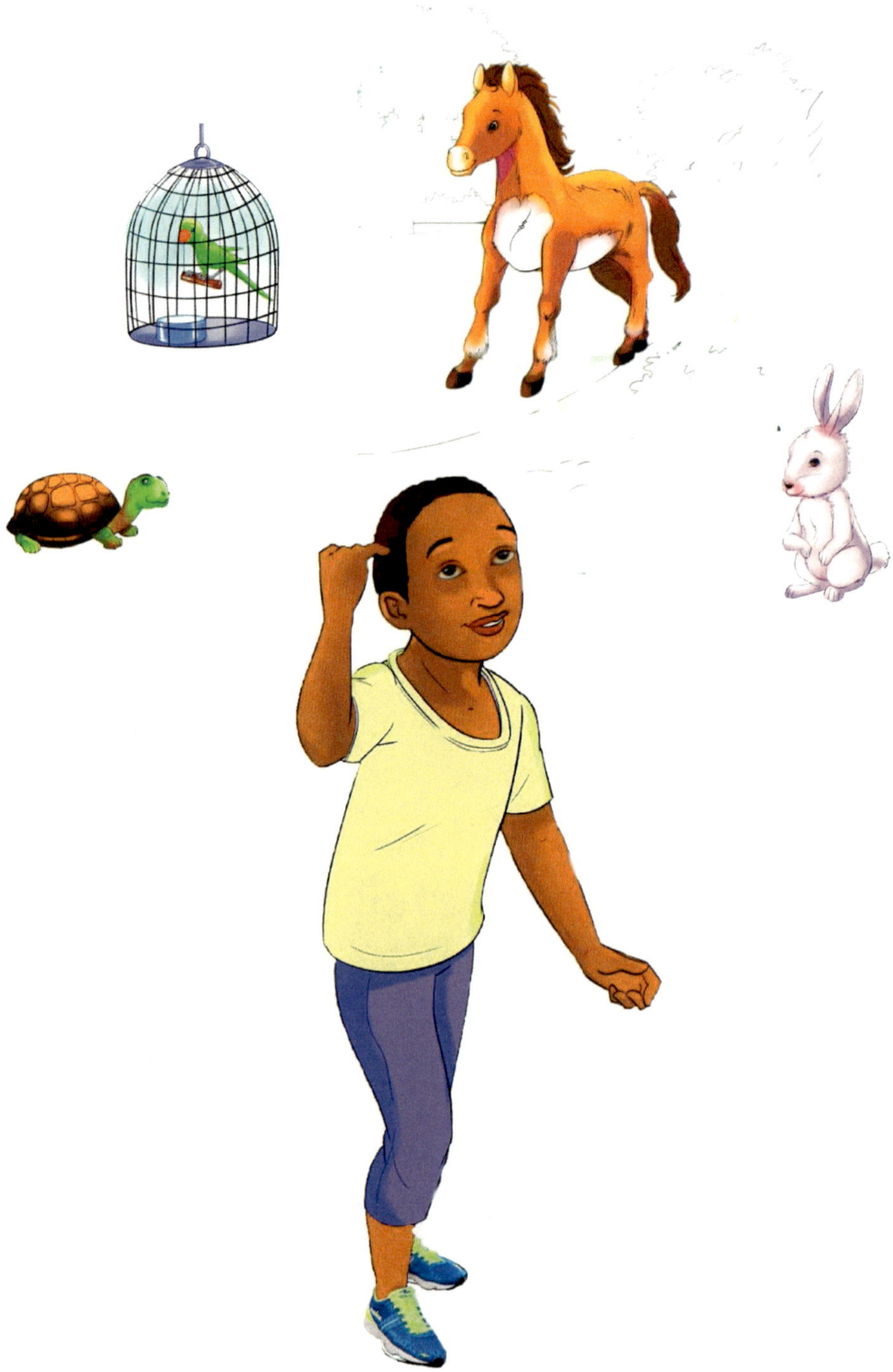

Mara and brothers, Kam and Ash, meet new friends, Vishnu and Indra. Join these happy children on a Saturday morning. They chat. Ash likes Indra's pet. Now, Ash wants a pet of his own. Will Ash get a pet?

In this story you will meet:

1. FRIENDS SAY HELLO

It is Saturday. Kam, Mara and Ash like Saturdays.

Eat now, said Mum and Dad.

They ate all!

Now Mara can go to see Kam and Ash play the pan.

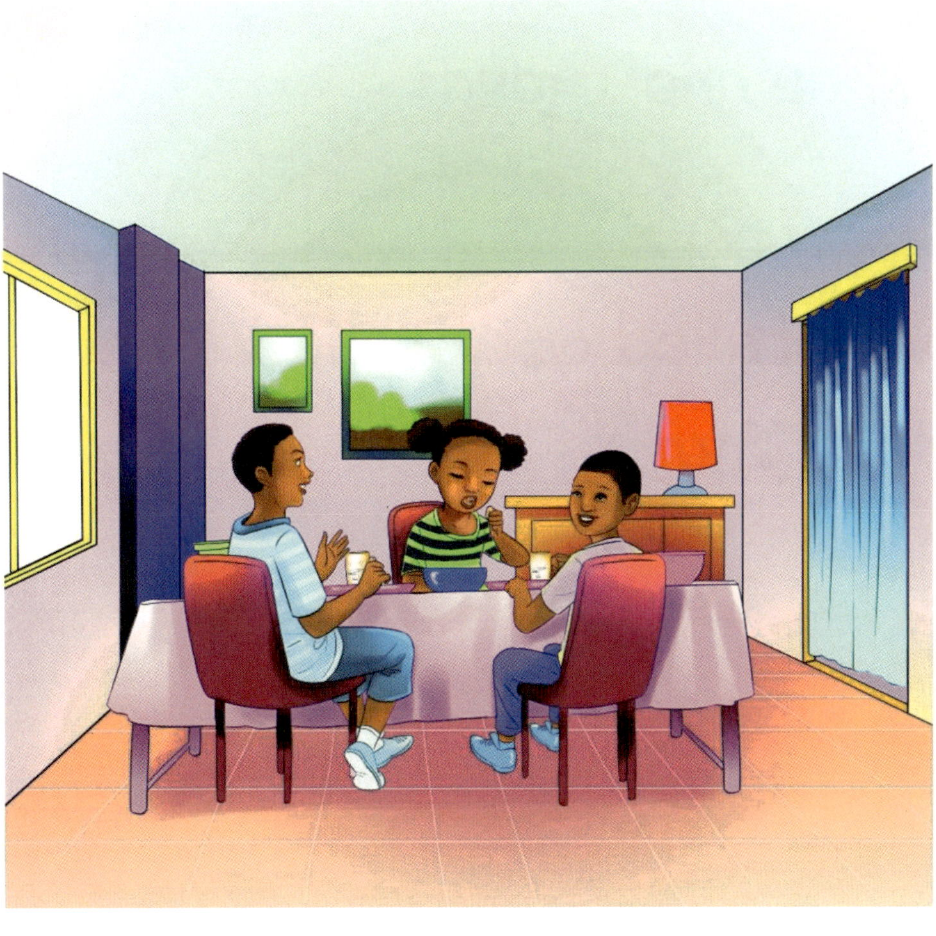

Sassy, the dog, is on a leash.

Mara sees a boy and a girl, Vishnu and Indra.

Mara called out, Hello Vishnu. Hello Indra.

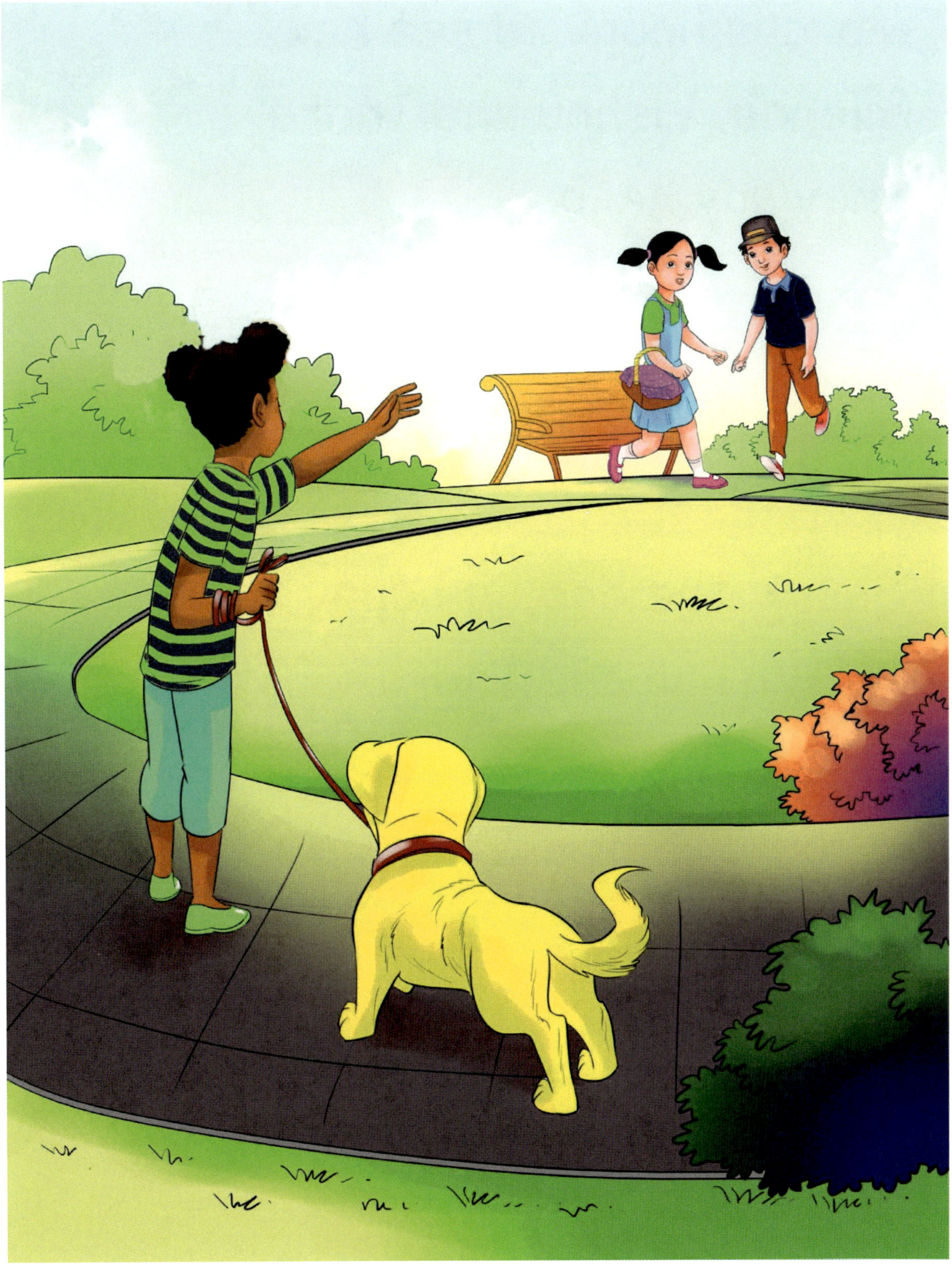

Mara is happy to see new friends, Vishnu and Indra. They say hello.

Indra pats Sassy.

Sassy, the dog, is happy to see Vishnu and Indra.

Sassy jumps and jumps.

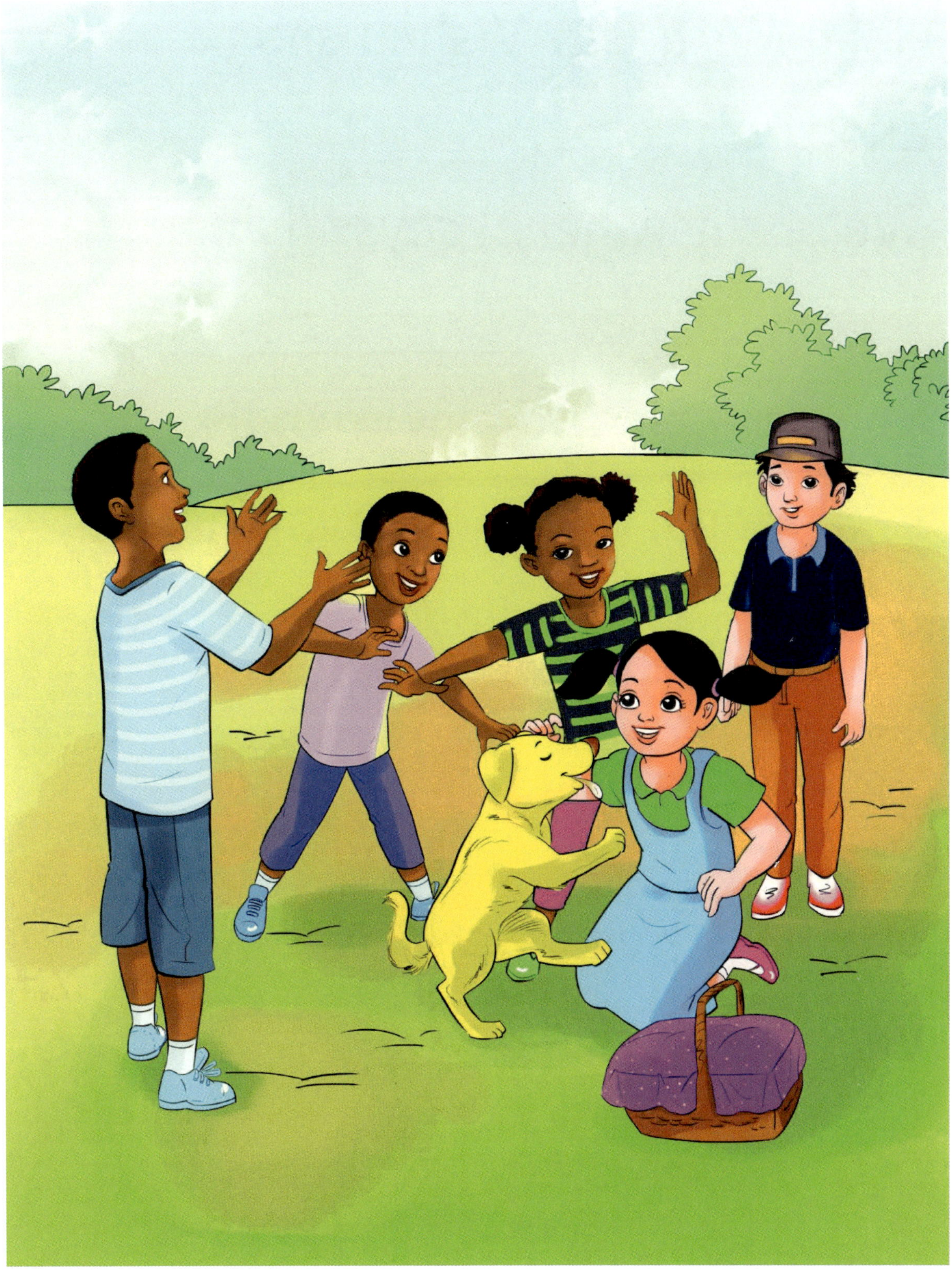

Hello Mara, say Vishnu and Indra.

We are new here, says Vishnu.

You can come to play with us, says Mara. Our house is the one with the yellow wall.

Kam and Ash are my two brothers, says Mara to Vishnu and Indra.

They say hello.

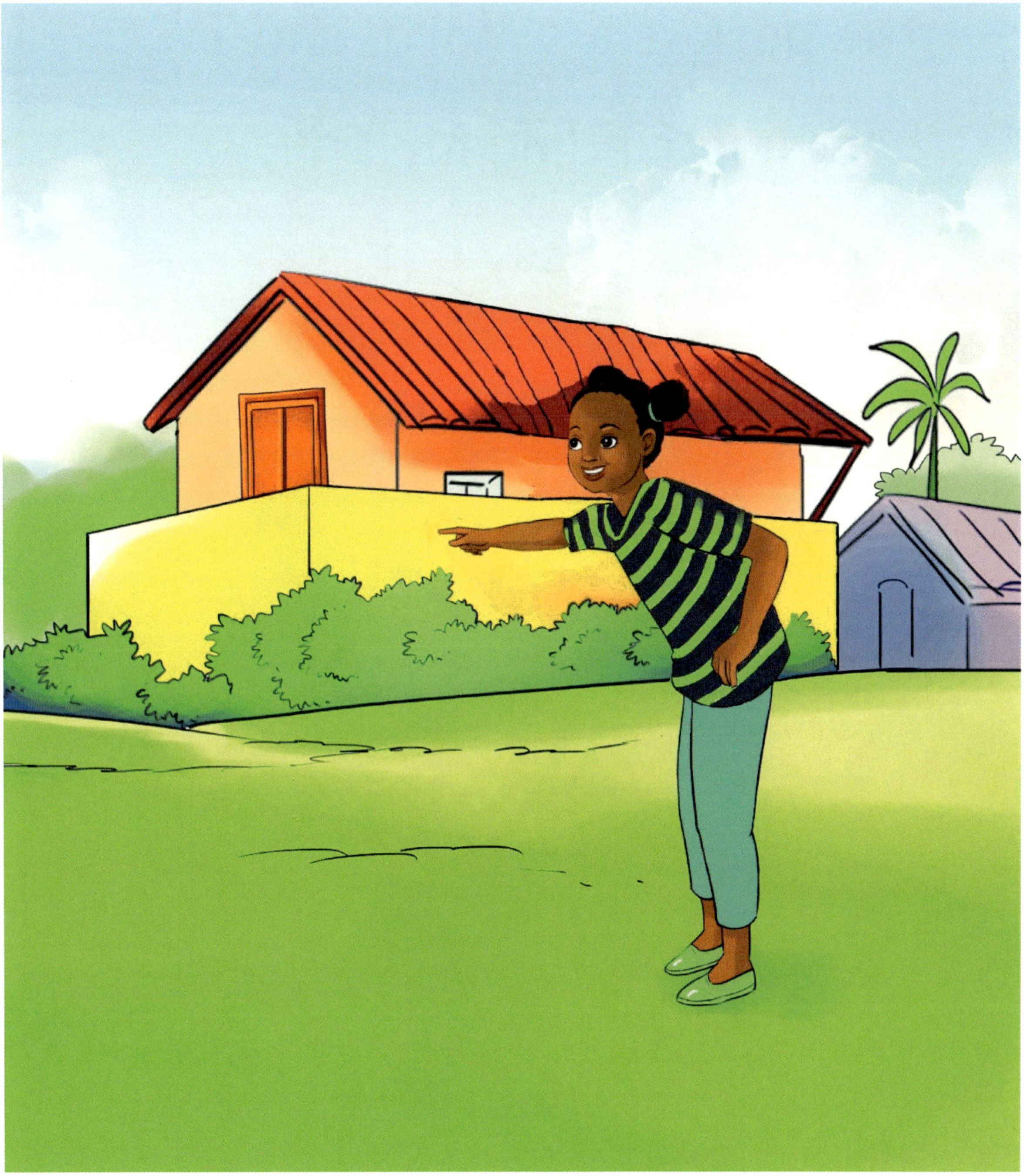

I saw Vishnu and Indra at the park, says Mara, and I had help finding my ball. Indra and Sassy got it.

Sassy wags and wags. Sassy likes Indra.

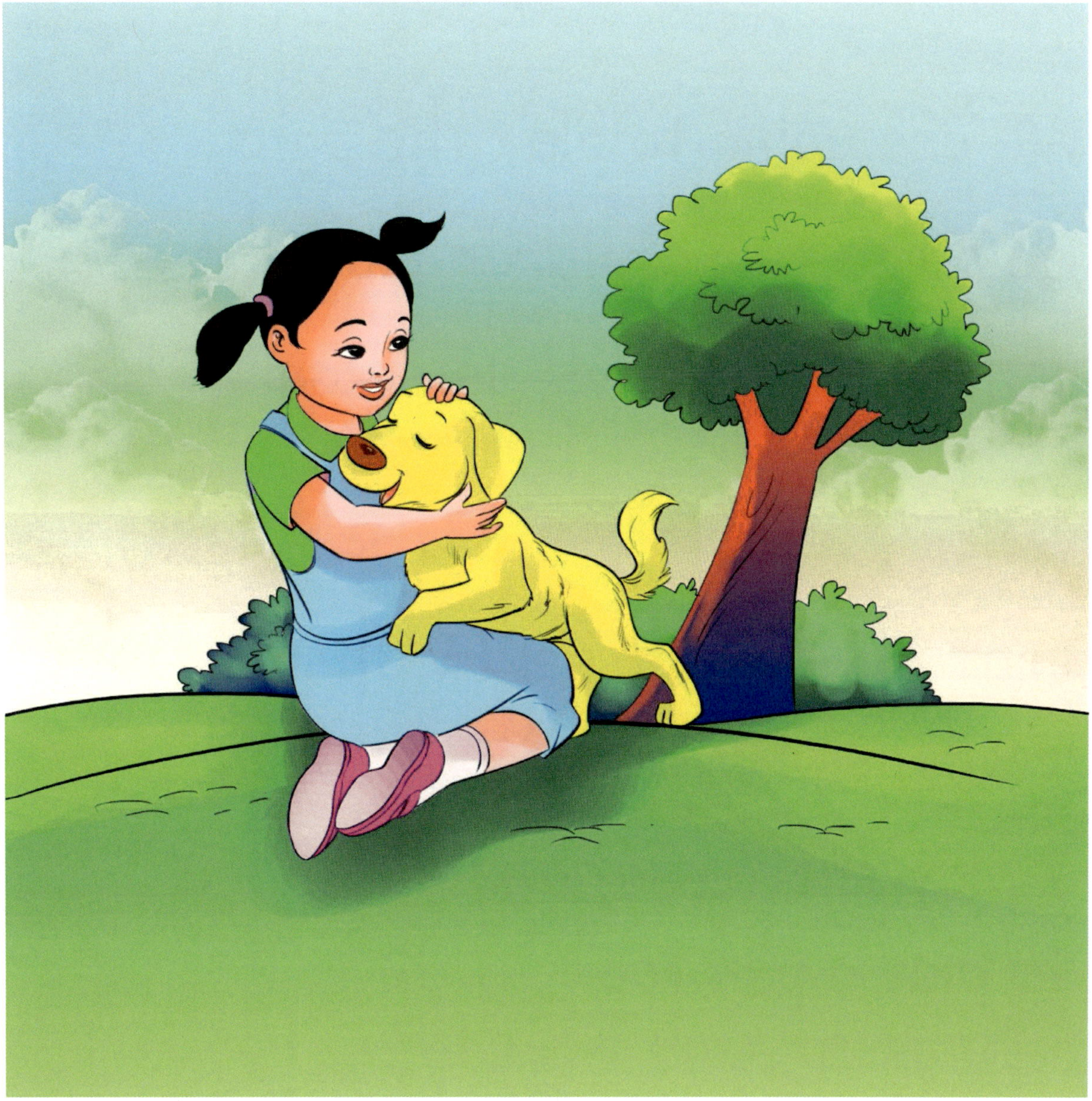

2. A Pet In A Basket

We are going to play the pans.
Do come too. Children play the
pans on Saturdays, said Kam.

That will be fun, said Vishnu.
I will ask my Dad.
I play the tassa, and I will like
to play a pan too.

A steel pan

A tassa drum

Indra has a basket.

Me-o-w. Meow. What is it? What's in the basket?

I have a pet kitten. She wants to see Kam and Ash play the pans too, says Indra.

They look down into the basket at the kitten. It looks like an all-white kitten, but they see two little brown ears.

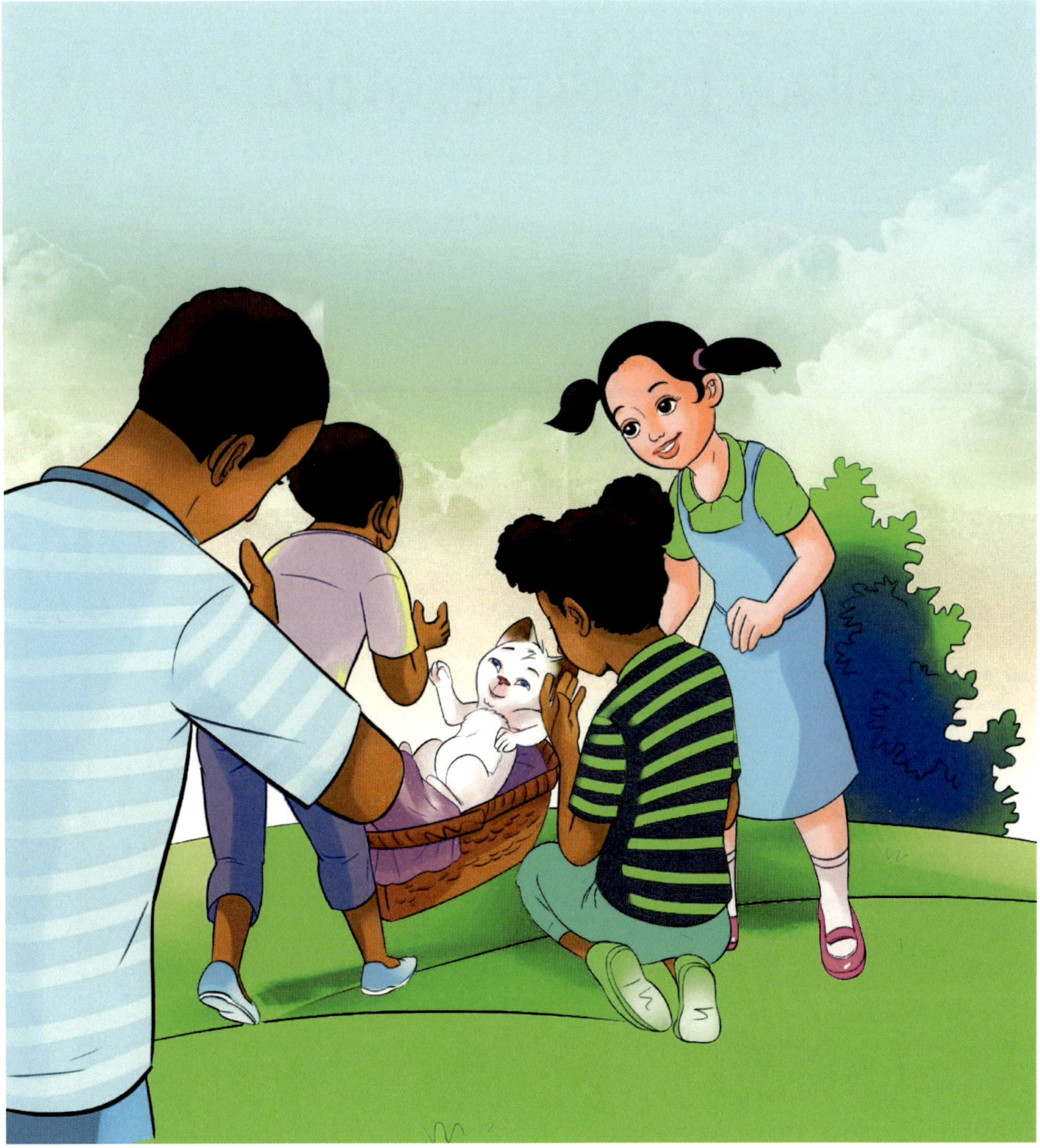

Mara pats the little kitten.

I call my pet kitten, Jazz, says Indra.

3. Kittens Are Fun

The kitten, Jazz, fits well in the brown basket. Ash pats the soft kitten.

Jazz is so soft and pretty, says Ash, I like the little brown ears.

Is she fun?

Kittens are fun. Jazz likes to play, says Indra.

Indra, we can play with the kitten, Jazz, and our four dolls, said Mara.

Mara and Indra are happy!

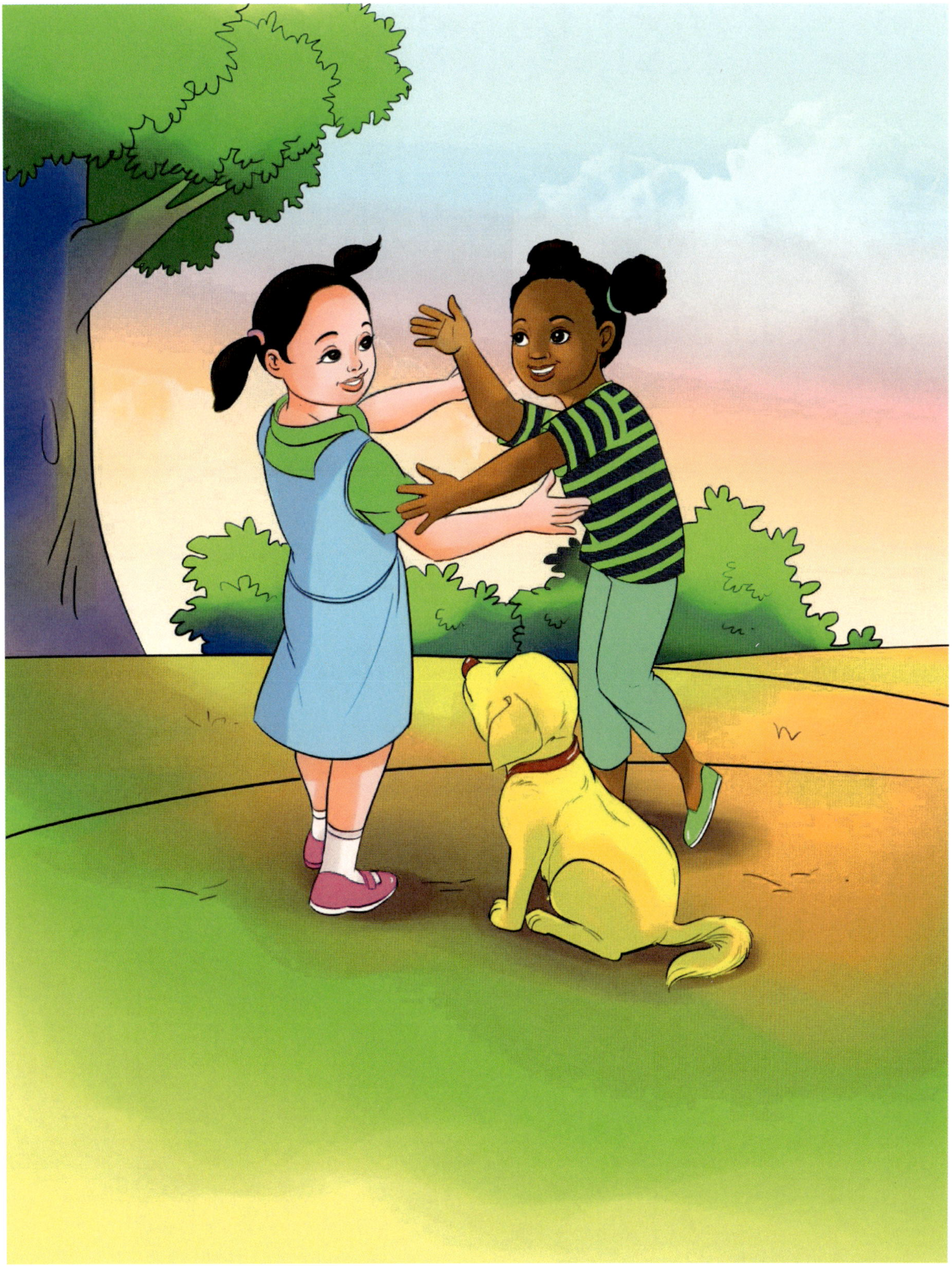

4. What Do Cats Like?

I have a black fish, says Kam. It's a Molly fish.

Jazz likes milk, says Indra. says Indra, but Jazz will soon get fish. Cats like fish!

Kam nods. He looks sad.
Yes, they do, he said.
You and Mara must play with Jazz, away, AWAY from my fish.

Kam gets a big hug.
We will, Kam, we will, said Mara.

Vishnu wants to play the pan with Kam and Ash next Saturday. Yes, he will ask his Dad and Mum.

5. Ash Wants A Pet

It is Tuesday. Ash is a bit sad.
Vishnu got a bird.

Ash tells Mum.

Mum, he says, I am a bit sad. Vishnu got a bird.

Kam has a fish.

Mara plays with Sassy.

Indra got a soft white kitten with brown ears!

May I please have a pet Mum?

Do you want a kitten too? asks Mum.
No, thank you Mum, I do not want a kitten, says Ash.

Mum, I want a pony that I can ride, says Ash.

Mum looks at Ash.

Now her eyes are big!

You want a pony, Mum says.

Ash nods.

... or a turtle, or a rabbit!

says Ash

May I please have a pet? Ash begs Mum.

Mum hugs Ash.

6. Ash Gets A Pet

It is Friday.

Who's there?
It's Dad, with a big box.

Good afternoon, Dad, says Ash.

Ash helped Dad to get the box to the table.

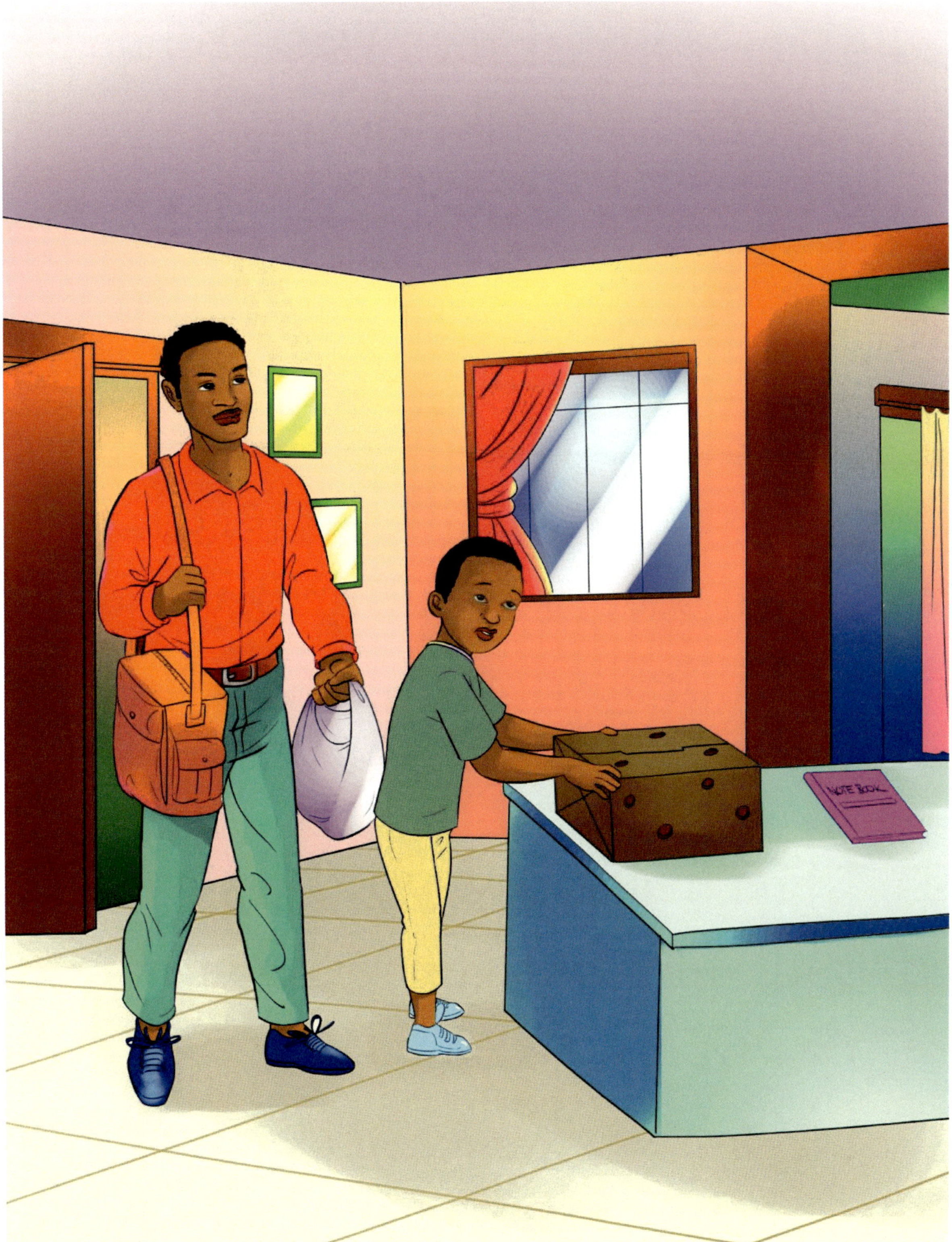
NOTE BOOK

How was school? asks Dad.

School was fun, Dad. Tim had his pet Pete, a parrot in a cage, for our Friday 'Show and Tell'.

Yes, I had a nice day, yet I am a bit sad. Dad, will I get my pet soon?

This is for you, Ash, says Dad.

Is the box for me?
What's in it, Dad? asks Ash.

You have a pet now, Ash, says Dad.

Ash was so happy.

Mum! says Ash, Dad is here.
He came home with my pet!

Ash ran to tell his Mum.

Come Mum! I got a pet!

I got a pet! said Ash.

Ash led Mum to the box.

Kam, Mara, please come now! I got a pet.

What is it? asks Kam. Did Dad get you a pony?

Is it a turtle or a rabbit? What is it Dad? I'm so happy! says Ash.

Ash looks in the box.
It is a turtle. Its head is under its shell.
Ash gets the brown and yellow turtle out of the box.

I will call him Tex, says Ash.

Look, he went under the table! Ash, I like this pet.
Yes, I do like Tex, says Mum.

Ash hugs Mum and Dad.
They get a huge hug.

Thank you, Dad.
Thank you, Mum, says Ash,
I am so happy!

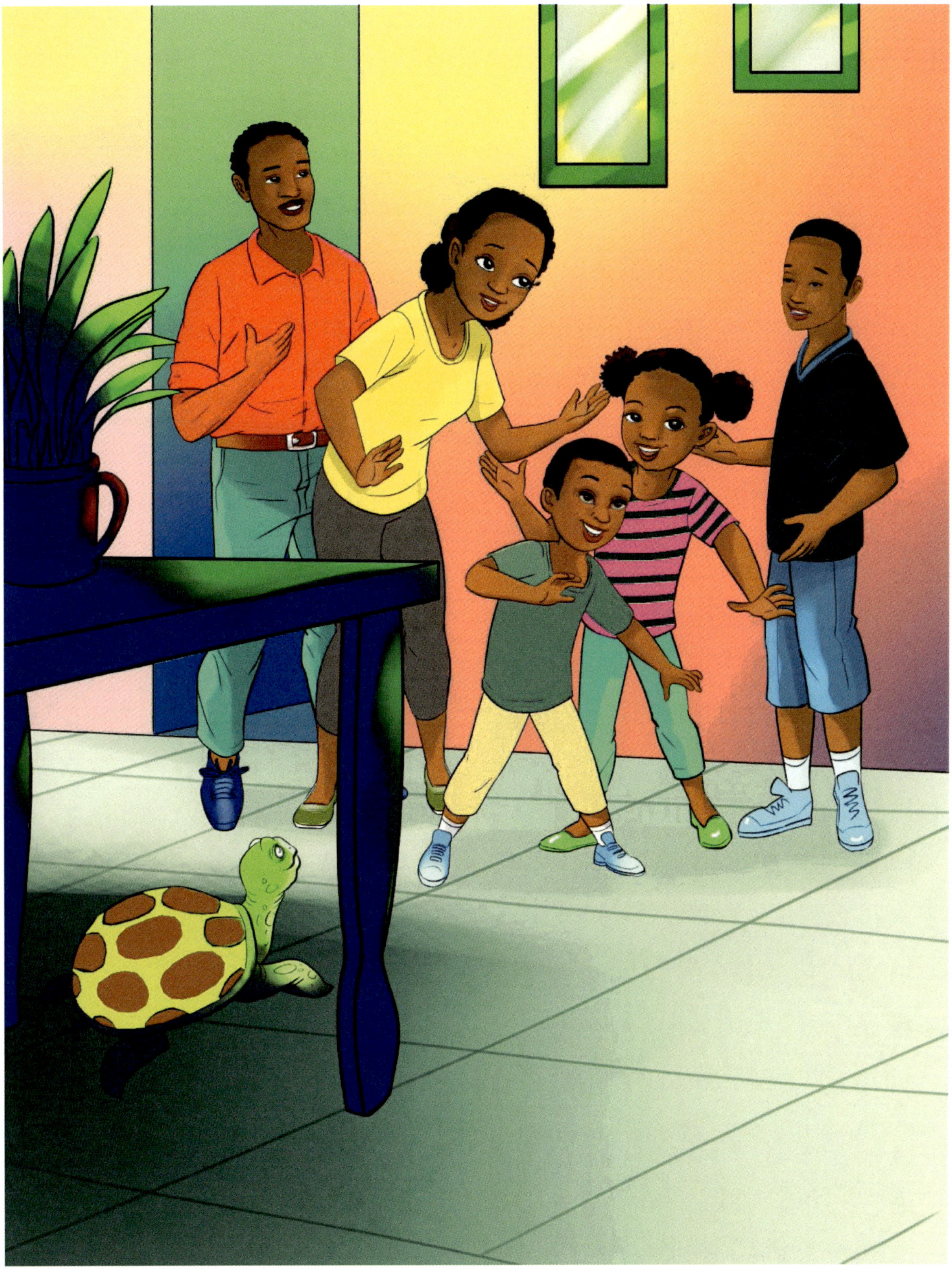

Units   Reading Comprehension

1. What did Mara and her brothers do on Saturdays?
   Why do you think Mara had Sassy on a leash?
   Where did Mara first meet Vishnu and Indra?

2. What musical instrument does Vishnu play?
   What do you know about the tassa and the steel pan?
   What does Indra have in her basket? Describe it.
   What sound does it make?

3. How does Mara wish to have fun with Jazz?
   Do you think having a kitten is fun? What would be your favourite pet?

4. What pet does Kam have? Does it have a special name?
   What colour is it? Why did Kam become unhappy? How did Mara respond? How would you have responded?

5. Which three pets did Ash have on his list?
   How did Mum respond when Ash asked for a pony?

6. How did Ash react to the good news from his Dad?
   How do you think Ash knew that he did **not** get a pony?
   Which pet did he get? Why do you think this pet sometimes puts its head under its shell?

   How did Ash show his Dad and Mum that he was so happy that he now had a pet?

Story Retelling

At the end of the story do a 'picture walk' with the class.

At each illustration, encourage active story discussion.

- Can they retell the story? Who was the main character?
- Where did the story take place?
- What happened at the beginning/ middle/ and end of the story.
- What did children learn from the story?

Speaking and Listening

Each child draws an illustration of a pet or a toy, real or fantasy, writing one sentence about it along with the beginning letter-sound of its name. Have them talk about their drawings in a class 'Show and Tell'. Display their illustrations on the class Notice Board.

Art: Make a **Thank You** card for Ash to give to his Mum and Dad.

Be Responsible

Teacher/Parent: Discuss the meaning of the word **responsible**. Ask: Why do dogs sometimes need to be on a leash?
This unit attempts to increase awareness of one's responsibility to demonstrate safety for others in the community. Discuss other ways by which responsible actions may be demonstrated e.g. not littering the streets, proper disposal of water bottles and juice boxes, not defacing property.
Have a **teacher/parent-led echo-reading of the rhyme** (with appropriate hand movement).

Be responsible!
It is up to you and me
To make Trinidad and Tobago,
The best that it can be!

Review of vc and cvc words

it mum dad can pan dog on pat us
at had got wag / fun in pet an but/ fit /
get cat nod sad yes big hug / bit not
beg / box yet ran led am/

Infants 1 Sight-Word Review

Unit 1: like eat now they ate all /
on out / new say / with our / are/
saw at
Unit 2: do too that will be /what /
have she want into / white but
brown
Unit 3: well so pretty/ four
Unit 4: black get / yes he must /
Unit 5: am / please was no / ride
Unit 6: who there good / soon / this
ran / came did/ went under

Pre-Primer Sight Word Review

it is and said to you can go the a see/
jump come play one yellow my help find /
we look in little down two/ not/ I for here me

> Review of the letter sounds /t/ and /d/, reinforcing word-sounds with inflectional ending /ed/ that are introduced at this reading level. This is a parent or teacher-led **Echo Reading** exercise with the child.

Tap and dance to Dan

With a pan-stick in each hand

Dan and the pan

are a one-man band!

/t/ /t/ /t/ tap tap tap and

/d//d//d/ dance dance dance,

We tap and dance to his music

All over the land.

> **Exercise: Is it a /t/ or a /d/ letter sound?** Listen carefully as you say each pair of words. How many of them have the 'ed' ending with a /d/ letter sound? How many have the 'ed' ending with a /t/ letter sound? Have fun doing this exercise!
>
> like/ liked   play/played   jump/ jumped   look/ looked   help/ helped   call/ called
>
> dance/danced

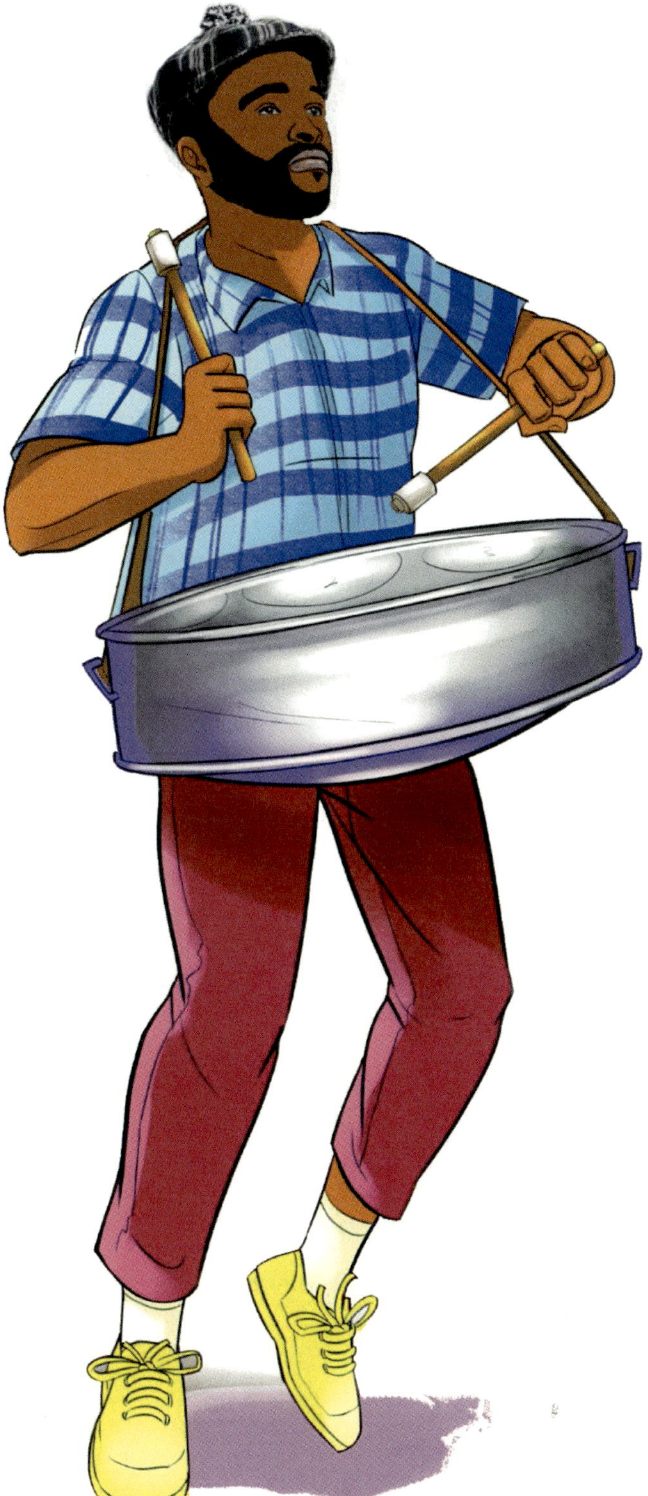

This book, Mara and Friends, continues to reinforce blending of **cvc** words using a children's story Ash Wants a Pet. These skills would have been acquired during their Pre-Primer reading of Mara and Friends.

The story Ash Wants A Pet, introduces all the basic *Dolch Sight-Words at the Infants 1 reading level, and reinforces recognition of some of the Pre- Primer Dolch Sight-Words that were learned as they read Mara and Friends 1. All **cvc** words and Infants 1 Dolch Sight-Words are listed for review p.43, in the order of their first use in this story. Punctuation marks introduced in Book 1 continue. They assist with fluency. Observe children's tone and pace during reading.

Illustrations also assist children to make connections, facilitating the use of context and picture clues as decoding strategies.

As children progress with Sight-Word recognition and with their decoding strategies, there is an increase in motivation and confidence. Observe and assist them during their periods of **Silent Reading**.

Read Aloud and **Echo-Reading** should also be included in scheduled Reading activities.

Discussion is an important component in group-reading of this story. Topics may include *Responsibility* (for example, having a dog on a leash in public spaces, and the teacher or parent-led Echo Reading of the poem **Responsibility** p.42); *Emotions*; *Introductions*; *Greetings*; *Showing appreciation*; *Musical Instruments*; and in *Science classes* - young animals, animal sounds and animal coverings.

Reading Comprehension questions are included on page 40. These help the child to make personal connections with what has been read in the story.

Make each reading experience an enjoyable one.

---

*Edward William Dolch, PhD (1889-1961) author of many children's stories and texts, first published the Dolch Word List in a journal article in 1936. He then published it in his book 'Problems in Reading' in 1948. The Dolch Sight Words have made the Reading process enjoyable for many children.

On successful completion of *Ash Wants A Pet*,
children should exhibit improved Reading Skills as they

- display appropriate listening and participatory skills during periods of reading and discussion
- demonstrate knowledge of letter sounds of the English alphabet individually and in text
- blend simple **cvc** words for reading
- demonstrate increased awareness (*does it sound right?*) of long and short vowel sounds in spoken single syllable words
  Final chapter words: c**a**ge   P**e**te   n**i**ce   h**o**me   h**u**ge
- demonstrate awareness of the differing pronunciations of some letters such as **c** and **g**. ni**c**e; **c**age
- identify words that rhyme with a given word e.g. call, wall, that rhyme with sight word **all**.
- read, in context, inflectional forms **'s'**, **'ing'**, **'ed'** (find**ing**, go**ing**, call**ed**, help**ed**) and words with contractions, e.g. It's
- recognize that some verbs have an irregular past tense
  e.g. sight words: see/saw, come/came, say/said.
- recognize that naming words may have irregular plural forms e.g. children.
- demonstrate awareness that some letter-sounds combine producing consonant blends at the beginning and end of words
- recognize that some words have more than one 'beat' or syllable.
- use context and picture clues to identify new words
- read stories that contain levelled Sight Word vocabulary, decodable **cvc** words and familiar words that are decodable by using context and picture clues
- recognize punctuation marks that assist them with improving fluency as they read
- compare/contrast experiences of characters in the story, with their own experiences
- make predictions as they read a story
- retell a story in proper sequence – beginning, middle and end.
- create a new ending to a story

About the Author.

Mrs. Claire Mark, a retired schoolteacher, taught at Primary and Secondary levels for close to forty years. She obtained outstanding results on completion of a formal course in the Teaching of Reading offered at the UWI School of Continuing Studies. This served to enhance her skills in this field, thus sparking her interest to produce appropriate and stimulating material for some of her adolescent students. On retirement she continued to assist even younger children, writing stories and rhymes that included levelled phonics, sight-words and situations to encourage active class discussion. This made the reading experience meaningful and enjoyable. These books are as a result of evolving interest over the years in promoting early literacy and good citizenship in children.

Made in the USA
Las Vegas, NV
18 August 2021